COMPLETE GUIDE TO QUAIL FARMING

Master Sustainable Techniques, Optimize Egg And Meat Production, Boost Profits, And Ensuring Healthy Flock Management

GIOVANNI MALAKAI

© [2024] [Giovanni Malakai]. All rights reserved.

Except for brief quotations included in critical reviews and certain other noncommercial uses allowed by copyright law, no part of this publication may be reproduced, distributed, or transmitted in any form or by any means, including photocopying, recording, or other electronic or mechanical methods, without the publisher's prior written permission. Write to the publisher at the address below, addressing your letter to the "Attention: Permissions Coordinator," requesting permission.

DISCLAIMER

This book's content is solely intended for informational and educational purposes. The author and publisher of this book make no express or implied representations or warranties of any kind regarding the completeness, accuracy, reliability, suitability, or availability of the information, products, services, or related graphics contained in it, even though every effort has been made to ensure their accuracy and dependability. You consequently absolutely assume all risk associated with any reliance you may have on such material.

The author's own experiences and studies serve as the foundation for the techniques and procedures covered in this book. They might not be appropriate for every circumstance or person. Before putting any advice or recommendations from this book into practice, readers should use their own discretion and take into account their unique situation. Consulting with qualified professionals who specialize in veterinary care and animal management is always a good idea. Any direct, indirect, incidental or consequential damages resulting from using or relying on the material in this book are disclaimed by the author and publisher. Any decisions made by the reader based on the information presented herein are at their own risk.

TABLE OF CONTENTS

CHAPTER ONE 13
  INTRODUCTION TO QUAIL FARMING 13
    COMPREHENDING QUAIL PRODUCTION 13
    ADVANTAGES OF RAISING QUAILS 14
    BEGINNING THE PROCESS OF QUAIL FARMING 16
    FREQUENTLY HELD MYTHS REGARDING QUAIL FARMING 17
    REASONS WHY QUAIL FARMING IS A SUCCESSFUL BUSINESS 18

CHAPTER TWO 21
  BEGINNING 21
    SELECTING THE APPROPRIATE QUAIL BREED 21
    ORGANIZING YOUR FARM FOR QUAIL 22
    RECOGNIZING THE NEEDS FOR QUAIL HOUSING 23
    GETTING REPUTABLE QUAIL STOCK 25
    BASIC EQUIPMENT AND TOOLS REQUIRED 26

CHAPTER THREE 29
  NUTRITION OF QUAILS 29
    KNOWLEDGE OF QUAIL DIETARY REQUIREMENTS 29
    FEEDING PROCEDURES FOR OPTIMAL DEVELOPMENT 30
    CREATING A BALANCED DIET FOR QUAIL 31
    TYPICAL NUTRITIONAL INADEQUACIES AND THEIR TREATMENTS 32
    ADDING VITAMINS AND MINERALS TO QUAIL DIETS 33

CHAPTER FOUR 35
  QUAIL MEDICAL CARE 35
    IDENTIFYING COMMON HEALTH PROBLEMS WITH QUAILS 35

    PREVENTIVE STEPS IN THE MANAGEMENT OF DISEASE 36

    PUTTING BIOSECURITY MEASURES INTO PRACTICE......................... 37

    QUAIL VACCINATION PROCEDURES 38

    INITIAL CARE AND MANAGEMENT OF QUAIL ILLNESSES 39

CHAPTER FIVE... 41

    INCUBATION AND BREEDING 41

    RECOGNIZING THE CYCLES OF QUAIL REPRODUCTION..................... 41

    CHOOSING BREEDING STOCK.. 42

    METHODS OF NATURAL VS. ARTIFICIAL INCUBATION 43

    CONTROL OF INCUBATION TEMPERATURE AND HUMIDITY 45

    INCUBATION AND RAISING QUAIL CHICKS.. 46

CHAPTER SIX 49

    PRACTICES FOR MANAGING QUAILS.. 49

    DAILY SCHEDULE FOR MAINTENANCE AND CARE 49

    TRACKING THE GROWTH AND DEVELOPMENT OF QUAILS................ 50

    EFFECTIVELY MANAGING FLOCKS OF QUAILS 52

    MAINTAINING DOCUMENTS AND MANAGING DATA 53

    MANAGING SEASONAL SHIFTS AND DIFFICULTIES............................. 54

CHAPTER SEVEN 57

    PRODUCTION OF QUAIL EGGS 57

    OPTIMIZING QUAIL EGG PRODUCTION.. 57

    MONITORING THE QUALITY OF QUAIL EGGS....................................... 58

    EGG COLLECTION AND HANDLING PRACTICES................................... 59

    PROMOTING QUAIL EGGS TO MAKE MONEY...................................... 61

    NOVELTIES IN THE PRODUCTION OF QUAIL EGGS 62

CHAPTER EIGHT 65
PROMOTING AND RETAILING QUAIL GOODS........................... 65
DETERMINE WHICH MARKETS TO TARGET WITH QUAIL PRODUCTS . 65
QUAIL PRODUCT PACKAGING AND BRANDING............................. 66
PRICING TECHNIQUES FOR QUAIL EGGS AND MEAT 68
CHANNELS OF DISTRIBUTION FOR QUAIL PRODUCTS.................... 69
MARKETING STRATEGIES FOR BUSINESSES THAT FARM QUAIL......... 71
CHAPTER NINE 73
COMPLIANCE WITH LAWS AND REGULATIONS......................... 73
COMPREHENDING QUAIL FARMING REGULATIONS 73
REQUIREMENTS FOR PERMITS AND LICENSES 74
OBSERVANCE OF SAFETY AND HEALTH REGULATIONS 75
CONSIDERING THE ENVIRONMENTAL IMPACT 76
RISK CONTROL AND INSURANCE FOR QUAIL FARMS 77
CHAPTER TEN 79
GROWING YOUR BUSINESS IN QUAIL FARMING......................... 79
INCREASING CAPABILITIES FOR QUAIL PRODUCTION 79
PARTNERSHIPS AND OUTSOURCING FOR DEVELOPMENT................ 80
EMPLOYING AND EDUCATING QUAIL FARM WORKERS.................... 82
BUDGETING AND FINANCIAL PLANNING 83
EXPANDING THE RANGE OF QUAIL GOODS AND SERVICES 84
CHAPTER ELEVEN 87
UPCOMING DEVELOPMENTS AND TRENDS 87
NEW TECHNOLOGY IN QUAIL PRODUCTION................................ 87
ECO-FRIENDLY METHODS FOR QUAIL FARMS............................... 88

    CONSUMER PREFERENCES AND MARKET TRENDS 89

    RESEARCH OPPORTUNITIES AND EDUCATIONAL INITIATIVES 91

    WORLDWIDE PROSPECTS FOR QUAIL FARMING ENTERPRISES 92

CHAPTER TWELVE 95

    FAQS & FREQUENTLY ASKED QUESTIONS 95

        TAKING CARE OF QUAIL EGGS 95

        TYPICAL QUAIL ILLNESSES AND THEIR TREATMENTS 96

        PROFITABILITY OF QUAIL FARMING FOR NOVICES 97

        IDEAL COMPOSITION OF QUAIL FEED 99

        EFFECTIVE QUAIL PRODUCT MARKETING 100

ABOUT THE BOOK

For those who want to start quail farming or expand their current operations, the "Complete Guide to Quail Farming" is a vital reference. This all-inclusive manual covers every facet of quail farming, from comprehending the fundamentals to managing legal and regulatory obligations, guaranteeing a complete and prosperous foray into this profitable sector.

Setting the scene, the introduction emphasizes the advantages of quail farming, busts myths, and shows why it's a worthwhile and successful endeavor. For novices, it offers a strong foundation, and for seasoned farmers, it is an invaluable resource.

"Getting Started," covers important topics such as selecting the best quail species, establishing the farm's infrastructure, and obtaining high-quality quail stock. For those who are just starting, this chapter serves as a road map that leads them through the first steps of setting up a profitable quail farm.

"Quail Nutrition" is equally important since it covers the dietary requirements of quails, feeding techniques for maximum growth, and approaches to creating balanced diets. It also addresses dietary inadequacies and supplementation, guaranteeing the well-being and efficiency of quail flocks.

Beyond basic care, the guide goes into "Quail Health and Care," where common health problems, preventive measures, biosecurity procedures, immunization schedules, and first aid for illnesses are covered. By taking a comprehensive approach, disease breakout risks are reduced and quail well-being is guaranteed.

The essentials of breeding and incubation—such as reproduction cycles, stock selection, incubation techniques, temperature control, and hatchling care—are thoroughly discussed. This chapter gives farmers the tools they need to successfully oversee breeding initiatives and maintain their quail herds.

"Quail Management Practices" provides information on flock management, growth monitoring, record-keeping, daily care schedules, and adjusting to seasonal obstacles. It gives farmers the resources they need to run successful, healthy quail farms all year long.

In quail farming, egg production is a substantial source of income and is covered in detail in the guide. To ensure farmers' profitability, it covers maximizing egg yield, quality control, collection and handling procedures, marketing tactics, and advances in egg production.

An important topic covered is marketing and selling quail products, which includes target market identification, branding, pricing strategies, distribution routes, and promotional activities. This chapter offers advice on how to contact your target market and increase sales for farmers.

Emphasis is placed on legal and regulatory compliance, which includes risk management, licensing, environmental concerns, and health requirements. This guarantees farmers follow industry standards and stay inside the law.

The topic of scaling the quail farming industry is examined, along with information regarding partnerships, staffing, financial planning, diversification, and expansion tactics. This chapter sets the stage for the quail farming industry's long-term expansion and sustainability.

The guide concludes by examining upcoming developments and trends, stressing global prospects, sustainable practices, market trends, educational possibilities, and developing technology. It keeps farmers up to date-and ready for changing business environments.

Common issues and often-asked questions are covered in the guide, offering helpful answers for handling quail eggs, controlling illnesses, determining profitability, creating optimal diets, and putting marketing plans into action.

CHAPTER ONE

INTRODUCTION TO QUAIL FARMING

COMPREHENDING QUAIL PRODUCTION

A specialized yet extremely lucrative agricultural endeavor, quail farming entails growing and rearing quails for a variety of uses. For those who want to start farming quail, it is essential to grasp the fundamentals of the industry. First and first, one must be aware of the various quail species that are good for farming, such as Japanese quails, which are well-liked for their quick growth and abundant egg production.

Second, it's critical to comprehend quail housing requirements. Quails do best in homes with enough ventilation, lighting, and bedding made of straw or sawdust.

It's also essential to understand the dietary requirements of quails. For them to grow and be productive, a well-balanced diet high in protein, vitamins, and minerals is essential.

Furthermore, understanding the quail's breeding and reproductive cycle is essential to quail farming. Quails can lay eggs all year round and attain sexual maturity in about 6 to 8 weeks. Comprehending the duration of incubation and the process of hatching is essential for effective breeding.

Furthermore, keeping a healthy flock of quail depends on being aware of prevalent health problems and preventive actions. A thorough cleaning regimen, immunization schedules, and routine health examinations are essential components of managing quail farms.

ADVANTAGES OF RAISING QUAILS

Quail farming is a lucrative endeavor that appeals to both novice and seasoned farmers due to its many advantages. First of all, quails develop more quickly than other poultry birds, maturing more quickly. For quail growers, this means faster returns on their investment. Second, quails lay a lot of eggs—some species can produce up to 300 eggs annually.

Because of their large egg yield, quail farming is a profitable enterprise, particularly in areas where there is a strong market for quail eggs. Furthermore, quails are suited for small-scale farming operations because they take up less space than larger poultry animals like chickens or turkeys.

Furthermore, quails are renowned for their resilience and environmental adaptability to a wide range of conditions. Because they require less upkeep and are less prone to disease, quail farmers can lower their overall operating costs.

Moreover, quail eggs and meat are regarded as being extremely nutrient-dense, having a high protein content and low cholesterol. Because of its high nutritional content, quail goods are more marketable and draw in health-conscious customers. All things considered, quail farming is a lucrative and sustainable agricultural endeavor because of its rapid development, high productivity, low maintenance, and nutritional value.

BEGINNING THE PROCESS OF QUAIL FARMING

Beginners must adhere to a few crucial measures to launch a profitable quail farm. First and foremost, it's critical to carry out in-depth research and learn about quail farming techniques. Understanding the market need, appropriate quail species, housing needs, feeding schedules, and health management techniques are all part of this. Secondly, it is important to establish the quail farm's infrastructure.

This entails building appropriate housing structures, like cages or pens, with enough lighting, ventilation, and sanitary facilities. Enough room must be allotted for each quail to guarantee their comfort and welfare.

Furthermore, it's critical to purchase quail from reliable providers in a healthy and high-quality stock. Quails that are immunized, disease-free, and the right age for breeding or egg production are the best choices for novices. Furthermore, the growth and production of quails depend on the development of a feeding regimen specifically designed to meet their nutritional needs.

Ensuring optimal health and egg production requires feeding a balanced diet consisting of commercial feeds supplemented with greens, grains, and protein sources. A prosperous start to quail farming requires routine monitoring of the health of the birds, the quantity of eggs produced, and general farm management.

FREQUENTLY HELD MYTHS REGARDING QUAIL FARMING

Despite all of its advantages, there are a lot of myths about quail farming that discourage newcomers from taking up this business. It's a popular belief that quails need large spaces and specific amenities, although this isn't quite accurate.

Because they can survive in small housing systems, quails are a good choice for backyard or small-scale farming operations. Another myth is that selling quail eggs is hard, even though demand for them is rising because of their high nutritious content and adaptability in the kitchen.

Furthermore, it's a common misconception that quail farming is labor-intensive and expensive, but this isn't always the case. Quail farming is a feasible and successful endeavor with the right preparation, know-how, and management.

There's also a myth that quails are easily sickened and need constant medical attention. Although precautions must be taken, quails are typically hardy birds that can tolerate a variety of environmental conditions with little harm to their health. It's critical to dispel these widespread myths to advance quail farming as a profitable and fulfilling agricultural endeavor.

REASONS WHY QUAIL FARMING IS A SUCCESSFUL BUSINESS

Several important aspects of quail farming make it a lucrative endeavor. First of all, female quails can lay eggs within 6 to 8 weeks of reaching adulthood, indicating a brief reproductive cycle. For quail growers, this quick egg output means quick returns on investment. Second, the poultry business can profit from the strong demand for quail eggs and meat because of their high nutritious content. Quail products are becoming more and more popular as health-conscious customers become more aware of their advantages.

Furthermore, quails require less space and resources than larger poultry birds, which lowers farmers' operating expenses. Reduced mortality rates and increased productivity are also a result of their hardiness and climatic tolerance.

Furthermore, integrating quail farming with other agricultural pursuits like vegetable growing or agro-tourism can help farmers diversify their sources of revenue. In addition, the demand for quail goods has surged because of the global movement towards sustainable and organic agricultural practices. This has given farmers the chance to capitalize on premium pricing and niche markets.

Quail farming is a lucrative endeavor for both novice and seasoned farmers because of its mix of quick returns, strong product demand, cheap operating costs, and sustainability. Resolving misunderstandings, capitalizing on market possibilities, and comprehending the subtleties of quail farming are essential tactics for success in this fulfilling farming venture.

CHAPTER TWO

BEGINNING

SELECTING THE APPROPRIATE QUAIL BREED

For quail farming to be successful, choosing the right species of quail is essential. While selecting the ideal species for your farm, there are several things to take into account. First, evaluate the habitat and climate in your area, as various quail species prefer distinct environments. For example, Coturnix quails can adapt to a wide range of conditions, whereas Japanese quails do better in warmer regions.

Second, think about the reason for your farm: is it to produce meat, eggs, or both? Every species has distinct qualities that fit them for particular uses. Because of their prolific egg-laying nature, Japanese quails are perfect for farms that produce eggs. However, Coturnix quails are prized for their high meat quality and quick growth rate, which makes them a good choice for meat production.

Finally, take local consumer tastes and market demand into account. Find out which quail species are in demand by conducting market research, then make your selection accordingly. An effective quail farming endeavor is built on the selection of the appropriate quail species based on climate appropriateness, farm purpose, and market demand.

ORGANIZING YOUR FARM FOR QUAIL

A quail farm needs to be carefully planned and must take many variables into account. Choose a decent starting point that has enough room, proper drainage, and easy access to sources of clean water. Environmental guidelines for farming operations and municipal zoning laws should also be followed by the area.

Next, build housing structures for quail that offer enough room, ventilation, and defense against predators. To guarantee the comfort and protection of the quails, think about utilizing wire mesh cages or enclosed aviaries with suitable flooring.

For effective farm management, install feeding and watering systems that are simple to access and maintain.

Put biosecurity measures in place as well to keep your flock of quail healthy and stop disease outbreaks. This includes keeping an eye out for any indications of illness or stress in the quails, as well as routinely cleaning and disinfecting the facilities and managing the trash. Successful quail farming operations are facilitated by establishing a quail farm with appropriate infrastructure, biosecurity protocols, and regulatory compliance.

RECOGNIZING THE NEEDS FOR QUAIL HOUSING

Your quail flock's welfare, production, and overall health are greatly dependent on the quality of its housing. Comprehending the distinct housing requirements of quails is crucial for achieving efficient farm management. Housing for quails must give them enough room to walk around, build their nests, and roost.

A few things to think about when building quail housing facilities are ventilation, insulation, lighting, and temperature management. Maintaining air quality and preventing moisture buildup inside dwelling structures require proper ventilation. Insulation aids in controlling temperature swings, particularly during severe weather.

Enough lighting must be provided to replicate the cycles of natural daylight, as this is essential for the reproductive and behavioral routines of quail. Controlling the temperature is essential to preventing heat stress and cold-related problems in quails, particularly in times of extreme weather. Include perches, roosting spaces, and nesting boxes in the housing structures to support the quails' natural needs and activities.

Maintaining clean, safe, and hygienic conditions that promote quail productivity and well-being requires routine inspections and upkeep of quail housing facilities.

You may establish a cozy and effective habitat for your quail flock to flourish by being aware of and attending to their unique housing demands.

GETTING REPUTABLE QUAIL STOCK

Getting high-quality quail stock is essential to your quail farming endeavors' success. Obtain quail chicks or mature quails from respectable hatcheries or breeders who have a track record of producing genetically sound and healthy stock. To find trustworthy suppliers, do extensive research and ask seasoned quail growers for advice.

Prioritize features including health, vitality, production, and desired attributes for the use of your farm while choosing quail stock.

Select quails with a history of high egg-laying rates and good reproductive performance, for instance, if your goal is egg production. If producing meat is your main objective, choose quails that have high meat yields and quick growth rates.

Make sure the quail stock you purchase is free of parasites, illnesses, or genetic flaws that could affect its performance and overall health. To stop illnesses or viruses from spreading among your current flock, quarantine incoming stock before integrating it. Regularly monitor and assess the health and condition of your quail stock to maintain a healthy and productive flock throughout time.

You may lay a solid basis for a prosperous and long-lasting quail farming business by obtaining high-quality quail stock from reliable suppliers and putting biosecurity measures in place.

BASIC EQUIPMENT AND TOOLS REQUIRED

Having the right tools and equipment for your quail farm is crucial to effective farm management and the best possible care for your birds. Invest in dependable, user-friendly tools and equipment that are appropriate for quail farming activities. Here are some fundamental instruments and equipment required for quail farming:

1. Cages or aviaries: Provide housing structures that offer ample space, ventilation, and safety for your quails. Depending on the size, temperature, and management techniques of your farm, select wire mesh cages or enclosed aviaries.

2. Feeding and watering systems: Install easily accessible, hygienic, and maintainable automatic or manual systems. Make sure your quails have a steady supply of clean water and fresh feed to encourage their growth.

3. Egg collection trays or nests: To make egg collection easier and avoid egg damage, use nesting boxes or trays made specifically for quail eggs. To promote consistent egg-laying behavior, give quails cozy and safe places to build their nests.

4. Heating and lighting equipment: To maintain ideal temperatures inside quail housing structures, take into account the use of heating lamps or bulbs, depending on your climate and surrounding conditions. To replicate

the natural daylight cycles for quail behavior and reproduction, use artificial illumination.

5. Cleaning and disinfection materials: To keep quail housing facilities clean and hygienic, stock up on cleaning supplies, disinfectants, and pest control solutions. Maintaining quail health and preventing illness outbreaks requires routine cleaning and disinfection of cages, equipment, and surrounding areas.

6. Purchasing instruments for safe handling of quails is recommended for doing chores like feeding, gathering eggs, and performing health examinations. Utilize monitoring instruments like egg candlers, humidity gauges, and thermometers to keep tabs on quail performance and environmental conditions.

You can increase output, improve quail welfare, and expedite farm operations by outfitting your quail farm with the right tools and equipment.

CHAPTER THREE

NUTRITION OF QUAILS

KNOWLEDGE OF QUAIL DIETARY REQUIREMENTS

There are particular nutritional needs for quails that are essential to their well-being and efficiency. Successful quail farming requires a fundamental understanding of these demands. Due to their omnivorous nature, quails can eat both plant and animal matter.

High-protein foods like worms, seeds, and insects should be a part of their diet to help them grow and lay eggs. For general health, they also need certain vitamins, minerals, and amino acids.

Including a range of items in their diet guarantees that kids get all the nutrients they need. For instance, a balanced diet can be achieved by serving greens like lettuce, spinach, and kale along with a mixture of grains like corn, millet, and sorghum. It's critical to keep an eye on their consumption and modify their diet as necessary to their stage of growth and overall health.

It is equally crucial to always have clean water available to promote digestion and avoid dehydration.

FEEDING PROCEDURES FOR OPTIMAL DEVELOPMENT

Achieving optimal growth in quails requires the use of appropriate feeding strategies. Feeding schedules ought to be standardized and adjusted for each stage of growth. Compared to adults, young quails need a diet higher in protein to maintain their fast growth.

Chicks should be fed starter diets with a protein content of about 24% to 28%, while layers can do well with feeds that have a protein content of 18% to 20%.

To prevent competition and congestion, feeding management also entails providing enough space for feeding. Hygiene standards are upheld when feeders made to reduce waste and keep feed clean are used. To avoid health problems, feeders should be cleaned regularly and any spoiled or tainted feed should be removed.

It is ensured that they receive the best nutrition possible for growth and productivity by keeping an eye on their feeding habits and modifying the feed mix in response to performance indicators.

CREATING A BALANCED DIET FOR QUAIL

Quail feed formulation requires knowledge of quail's nutritional needs and sourcing of high-quality ingredients. To satisfy their high protein requirements, quail feed usually consists of protein sources such as fish meal, soybean meal, or meat and bone meal.

Grain blends like corn, wheat, and millet give you energy, and adding vitamins and minerals keeps you healthy all around.

The nutritional content of the feed is increased by using premixes or supplements that provide important elements including calcium, phosphorus, and vitamins A, D3, and E. To get the right amounts of protein, fat, fiber, and moisture in the feed, precise formulation is needed.

Maintaining balanced diets requires routinely assessing feed quality and modifying formulations in response to nutritional analysis and quail performance.

TYPICAL NUTRITIONAL INADEQUACIES AND THEIR TREATMENTS

Several nutritional deficiencies can affect quails and affect their productivity and overall health. Deficiencies in calcium, phosphorus, vitamin D, and certain amino acids are common. Deficits can show up as aberrant feathers, weak bones, poor development, and decreased egg production. It is imperative to swiftly address these inadequacies to avoid future issues.

Supplements or feeds supplemented with the lacking nutrients can be added to the diet as a remedy for nutritional deficiencies.

To promote robust eggshells and bone health, for instance, calcium deficits can be corrected by supplementing feed with calcium carbonate or oyster shell.

Deficits can be successfully identified and addressed with the assistance of poultry nutrition specialists and routine quail health monitoring.

ADDING VITAMINS AND MINERALS TO QUAIL DIETS

It is imperative to include vitamins and minerals in quail meals to sustain their well-being and efficiency. Vitamins are essential for immunity, metabolism, and the development of eggs. Vitamin D3 is important for calcium absorption and bone health; vitamin E is an antioxidant; and vitamin A is important for vision and immune system function.

Minerals like calcium, phosphorus, and potassium are essential for the growth of the skeleton, the operation of muscles, and the creation of eggshells. Quails are guaranteed to consume enough minerals if mineral supplements are made available to them or if they are fed diets high in minerals. The dietary balance and general health of quail are best achieved by routinely evaluating and modifying supplementation based on nutritional analysis and quail performance.

CHAPTER FOUR

QUAIL MEDICAL CARE

IDENTIFYING COMMON HEALTH PROBLEMS WITH QUAILS

Like any other livestock, quails might have a variety of health problems that could compromise their well-being and output. Quail farmers must be aware of these prevalent health problems to guarantee prompt treatment and stop large-scale epidemics. Respiratory infections are among the most prevalent health issues in quails, and they can be brought on by bacteria, viruses, or fungi. Sneezing, coughing, nasal discharge, and difficulty breathing are among the symptoms. Infestations of parasites like worms and mites are also common and can cause weight loss, decreased egg production, and loss of feathers.

Farmers need to regularly check on the health of their flocks of quail to properly treat these health issues. This entails examining the birds to look for any indications of disease or anomalies, such as lethargy, strange droppings, or decreased appetite. Furthermore, keeping the atmosphere tidy and sanitary is crucial to stopping the spread of illnesses among quails. Quails' risk of health problems can be greatly decreased by routinely cleaning and sanitizing the living area, giving them clean water and a balanced diet, and making sure they have adequate ventilation.

PREVENTIVE STEPS IN THE MANAGEMENT OF DISEASE

Implementing several preventive measures is part of a proactive approach to disease prevention in quail farming. Quarantine and biosecurity procedures for newly arrived quail are important aspects. Farmers can lower the risk of disease introduction by observing fresh birds for any indications of illness throughout their designated period of quarantine before reintroducing them to the main flock. Strict biosecurity protocols, such as limiting farm access, cleaning footwear and equipment, and managing wild bird populations nearby, can also aid in preventing the spread of disease.

Keeping quails' diets healthy and balanced is another protective measure. Giving them wholesome food that satisfies their nutritional needs boosts their immune systems and increases their resistance to illness. Additionally crucial to the prevention of disease are regular immunization programs. Speak with a veterinarian to create a vaccination program that is customized to the unique requirements of your quail farm and covers common illnesses like coccidiosis and Newcastle disease. Farmers may guarantee the general health of their quail flocks and drastically lower the likelihood of disease outbreaks by combining these preventive techniques.

PUTTING BIOSECURITY MEASURES INTO PRACTICE

To stop infections from being introduced into and spreading throughout quail flocks, biosecurity is an essential component of quail farming. The first step in putting in place efficient biosecurity measures is to create stringent entrance procedures for people, vehicles, and equipment coming onto the farm.

This comprises footbaths with disinfectants, defined entry locations, and protective gear for agricultural laborers. Reducing the number of guests and managing farm access can also help to reduce the chance of disease transmission.

Additionally, biosecurity must keep the quail housing area tidy and organized. It is helpful to get rid of possible disease vectors by routinely cleaning and sanitizing the environment, including the feeders, waterers, and nesting places. Reducing the number of wild birds and pests on the farm can also lower the chance of spreading disease. Furthermore, to prevent disease outbreaks and maintain the general health of quail flocks, biosecurity measures such as appropriate waste management and the biosecure disposal of deceased birds are essential.

QUAIL VACCINATION PROCEDURES

Vaccination is an essential part of quail farming to avoid financial losses and prevent birds from infectious diseases.

Finding the most common diseases in the area and speaking with a veterinarian to figure out the right shots and when to give them are the first steps in creating a thorough immunization schedule. Vaccines against infectious bronchitis, coccidiosis, and Newcastle disease are frequently administered to quails.

Vaccinate birds based on prescribed schedules, taking into account their age, stress levels, and danger of current diseases. To avoid infection and guarantee vaccine efficacy, adhere to stringent hygiene precautions when receiving a vaccination. Keep thorough records of the vaccination history for every individual or flock of birds, and keep an eye out for any negative reactions in vaccinated birds. To ensure optimal protection, examine and adjust immunization protocols regularly depending on veterinary advice and disease trends.

INITIAL CARE AND MANAGEMENT OF QUAIL ILLNESSES

Treating quail illnesses and reducing their negative effects on flock health requires prompt and efficient first aid and treatment procedures. Start by becoming aware of typical ailments that quail experience, along with their symptoms, such as wounds, respiratory infections, and dietary inadequacies. Maintain a fully supplied first aid kit that includes bandages, disinfectants, and veterinarian-recommended drugs.

To avoid subsequent infections, give sanitation and hygiene top priority when treating quail diseases. Apply treatments or medications as prescribed by a veterinarian, being careful to adhere to dosage guidelines and withdrawal times for any drugs given to food-producing birds. To stop the spread of illness or other birds' aggressiveness, separate sick or damaged birds from the rest of the flock. Keep a watchful eye on the course of treatment, and in cases that are difficult or severe, seek professional veterinary aid. To guarantee the greatest results for quail health and welfare, examine and update first aid techniques regularly based on experience and input from veterinary specialists.

CHAPTER FIVE

INCUBATION AND BREEDING

RECOGNIZING THE CYCLES OF QUAIL REPRODUCTION

Similar to many other birds, quail has distinct reproductive cycles that are essential to comprehend to successfully breed. In ideal weather circumstances, spring and summer correspond with their reproductive season. Quail exhibited enhanced mating behavior during this period, with males frequently engaging in complex courtship rituals to entice females. Comprehending these cycles assists breeders in devising efficient breeding schemes.

Quail begin their reproductive cycle with courtship and mating, during which the males perform displays to draw the females. After mating, females lay eggs within a few days, usually in nests protected by foliage. Quail eggs require precise temperature and humidity control during the 17–18 day incubation phase for the embryo to develop.

Chicks are precocial after hatching, which means that they can feed themselves not long after birth and are comparatively independent.

Understanding when these reproductive cycles occur and creating ideal conditions for mating, egg laying, incubation, and raising chicks are essential to successful breeding. Breeders can maximize the health and productivity of their flock of quail by coordinating breeding activities with natural cycles and giving each stage the care and attention it needs.

CHOOSING BREEDING STOCK

It is crucial to select a quality breeding stock to sustain robust and healthy quail populations. Breeders should take into account various aspects, including age, health, genetic variety, and desirable features, when choosing birds for breeding. For breeding programs, young, healthy birds with strong genetic backgrounds are best since they have a higher chance of producing healthy offspring.

To avoid inbreeding and preserve the general health and vitality of the flock, genetic variety is essential. To guarantee a broad gene pool and minimize genetic disorders, breeders should refrain from choosing closely related birds. Furthermore, choosing birds with desirable qualities like robust immunity, high egg production, and amiable disposition enhances the flock's overall quality.

Frequent health examinations and breeding stock monitoring are required to identify and quickly resolve any possible problems. Breeders may guarantee the long-term viability and sustainability of their quail farming enterprises by choosing and caring for wholesome, genetically diversified breeding stock.

METHODS OF NATURAL VS. ARTIFICIAL INCUBATION

There are benefits and drawbacks to both natural and artificial methods for incubating quail eggs. To replicate the natural process, broody chickens are allowed to sit on and hatch eggs during natural incubation.

Because it uses less equipment, this method can be practical, but it depends on finding broody chickens that are willing to reliably incubate eggs.

Contrarily, artificial incubation uses incubators to regulate humidity and temperature to promote the best possible growth of eggs. With this technology, breeders have better control over the incubation conditions and can modify the parameters to suit their needs. To guarantee correct operation, nevertheless, incubation equipment must be purchased, and regular monitoring is necessary.

The availability of broody hens, the size of the operation, and breeder preferences are some of the elements that influence the decision between natural and artificial incubation. Both approaches can be successful if managed carefully, with a focus on maintaining stable incubation conditions and monitoring egg development attentively.

CONTROL OF INCUBATION TEMPERATURE AND HUMIDITY

Proper temperature and humidity management are crucial during incubation to support the proper development of quail embryos. Quail eggs require stable temperatures ranging from 99 to 101 degrees Fahrenheit during the incubation period. Fluctuations outside this range can influence embryo development and hatch rates dramatically.

Another important factor is humidity; for quail eggs, the ideal relative humidity range is usually between 50% and 60%. Humidity levels that are too high or too low might lead to difficulties such as malpositioned embryos, dehydration, or excessive moisture in the incubator. For incubation to be effective, humidity levels must be regularly monitored and adjusted based on the stages of egg development.

To guarantee ideal circumstances, breeders should utilize high-quality incubators with precise humidity and temperature controls.

Crucial procedures for the successful incubation of quail eggs include routinely inspecting and calibrating incubation equipment and adhering to advised guidelines for controlling humidity and temperature.

INCUBATION AND RAISING QUAIL CHICKS

Quail eggs usually hatch in a few hours to a day after they have finished their incubation. Precocial chicks are born with their eyes open, all of their feathers, and the ability to move about and feed themselves not long after birth. It is the responsibility of breeders to provide their freshly hatched chicks with a safe, dry, and warm habitat.

After hatching, chicks should be closely examined for health and vitality. A balanced diet high in protein and other necessary elements promotes normal development and growth.

Maintaining hygiene and preventing disease requires clean water, suitable bedding, and routine cleaning of the brooder environment.

To get the best possible outcome, breeders need also to take into account elements like the need for space, protection from predators, and social interactions between chicks. Early chick development requires careful attention and supervision, which lays the groundwork for future healthy quail growth and productivity.

CHAPTER SIX

PRACTICES FOR MANAGING QUAILS

DAILY SCHEDULE FOR MAINTENANCE AND CARE

A reliable daily care and maintenance schedule is essential for a profitable quail farming enterprise. This schedule entails caring for your quail, feeding it, giving it water, and keeping an eye on its health.

Check your quail's feed and water supplies first thing in the morning. Make sure they have access to enough food and clean water to meet their nutritional requirements. Due to their voracious eating habits, quails should have regular food intake checks. To provide hygienic conditions and avoid contamination, periodically clean and replenish water and feed containers.

Examine your quail's living quarters next. To stop the accumulation of moisture and droppings, which can cause bacterial development and illnesses, clean the bedding material in their living space.

To keep your quail's habitat dry and clean, change the bedding regularly.

Lastly, take note of your quail's behavior and overall health. Keep an eye out for any symptoms of disease or discomfort, such as fatigue, strange excretions, or breathing problems. If there are any health issues, take care of them right away by seeing a veterinarian. Take proactive steps to protect your quail flock by keeping an eye out for potential threats such as pests and predators.

TRACKING THE GROWTH AND DEVELOPMENT OF QUAILS

To maintain the general health and production of your quail, you must keep an eye on their growth and development. To evaluate their nutritional status and general well-being, monitor their developmental milestones, including as weight gain and feather development.

Weigh your quail regularly to track their development. Over time, a healthy quail should gain weight steadily.

To make sure they get the nutrients they need for the best possible growth and development, modify their diet appropriately.

Keep an eye on your quail's feather growth, particularly during molting seasons. Quail naturally lose their old feathers during molting and grow new ones in their place.

During molting times, give them extra nourishment to help with feather renewal and to keep them healthy overall.

Keep an eye on your quail's reproductive health, particularly if you're raising them to produce meat or eggs. To evaluate the success of your breeding effort, monitor hatchability, fertility, and egg production rates. Optimizing reproductive success requires adjusting environmental parameters like temperature and illumination.

EFFECTIVELY MANAGING FLOCKS OF QUAILS

The secret to increasing production and profitability in quail farming is effective flock management. Put tactics into place to make the most of your quail flock's housing, feeding, breeding, and health care procedures.

Provide your quail with a well-designed housing system that offers enough room, ventilation, and sanitary facilities.

Divide your quail flock into appropriate age or breeding groups to improve management and minimize stress. Regularly clean and disinfect household places to prevent the spread of diseases and parasites.

Create a feeding schedule based on the dietary needs of your quail at various growth stages. For the best possible egg production and meat quality, provide a balanced diet that includes feeds high in protein. To minimize waste and guarantee effective feed conversion, keep an eye on feed consumption and modify rations as necessary.

Establish a breeding program to choose prolific and healthy quail for procreation. Keep an eye on hatchability, chick survival, and fertility rates to gauge the effectiveness of your breeding activities. To enhance desired qualities in your flock of quail, take into account genetic selection and crossbreeding techniques.

MAINTAINING DOCUMENTS AND MANAGING DATA

Effective data administration and record-keeping are crucial for quail farming to be successful. To monitor performance and make wise management decisions, keep thorough records of all important data, including feeding schedules, health status, egg production, hatch rates, and expenses.

Establish a system for keeping records that arranges data in an understandable and accessible manner. Record data systematically and regularly using digital tools or conventional paper-based techniques. For every record entry, include pertinent information such as the date, time, observations, and actions performed.

Examine and evaluate collected data regularly to find trends, patterns, and areas where your quail farming business needs to improve. Utilize data insights to improve overall productivity and efficiency, modify management procedures, and allocate resources optimally.

To work well together and make informed decisions, share pertinent data with stakeholders like farm managers, nutritionists, and veterinarians. Put in place data security procedures to safeguard private data and guarantee that privacy laws are followed.

MANAGING SEASONAL SHIFTS AND DIFFICULTIES

Throughout the year, quail farming requires adaptation to seasonal changes and obstacles to maintain maximum output and profitability.

Be ready for seasonal changes in the lightest and darkest hours of the day, the weather, and the surrounding environment that can affect quail performance and health.

Provide your quail flock with enough shade, ventilation, and cooling devices during hot weather to keep them from being overheated. To reduce heat-related problems, provide cooled water and modify feeding timings. During heatwaves, keep a close eye on the behavior and health of quail and respond quickly to reduce dangers.

To keep quail warm and cozy throughout the winter, insulate living places and add extra heating. Employ bedding materials that minimize drafts and maintain heat to avoid respiratory issues and stress brought on by the cold. During the winter months, modify feeding practices to suit increasing energy requirements.

Control egg production's seasonal variations by making the most of dietary supplements and illumination schedules. To encourage quail to produce eggs on shorter days, use artificial illumination to simulate extended daylight hours. Modify diet plans to include nutrients that are necessary for healthy reproduction and egg production.

Make backup preparations in case of severe weather that could interfere with regular farming operations, such as storms, floods, or droughts. To protect your quail flock and infrastructure, put emergency measures for shelter, evacuation, and resource conservation into practice.

CHAPTER SEVEN

PRODUCTION OF QUAIL EGGS

OPTIMIZING QUAIL EGG PRODUCTION

The first step in maximizing quail egg yield is to start with healthy, well-fed quails. Make that their nutrition is well-balanced and abundant in protein, vitamins, and minerals.

Enough room for the quails to walk around comfortably and nest boxes for laying eggs are also necessary for proper housing. Maintaining ideal environmental parameters, like as lighting and temperature, is important for reliable egg production.

To spot problems early, quail health and egg production must be regularly monitored. Keeping the quail housing area clean and hygienic is important for illness prevention and maintaining a healthy atmosphere. For further benefit, think about adding natural supplements to improve quail immunity and egg quality, such as probiotics or herbs.

Optimizing the quantity of eggs produced can also be achieved by carefully controlling the quail's breeding and laying cycles. One way to increase egg production is to mimic seasonal changes in lighting.

Egg yield is further increased by using proper egg collection techniques, such as gathering eggs several times a day to avoid breaking them and making sure they are clean and undamaged. To maximize quail egg yield, a combination of good diet, housing, health monitoring, and breeding management approaches is essential.

MONITORING THE QUALITY OF QUAIL EGGS

Quality control is crucial in ensuring that quail eggs satisfy high requirements for freshness, cleanliness, and safety. To ensure that quails lay high-quality eggs, start by giving them clean nesting materials and making sure they have access to clean water and food. To preserve quality, check eggs frequently for cracks or other anomalies, and discard any soiled or broken eggs right away.

It is essential to use appropriate egg-handling procedures. To avoid infection, wash eggs only when necessary using clean, sterilized equipment. Eggs should be kept cold and dry, ideally in a refrigerator, to maintain freshness and increase shelf life. Dates of manufacture on egg labels make it easier to monitor freshness and guarantee that consumers get high-quality goods.

Use suitable packaging materials that shield eggs from deterioration and temperature changes to preserve egg quality throughout storage and transportation. Regular quality inspections during the production and distribution process facilitate the early detection and resolution of any problems. You may make sure that quail eggs fulfill consumer expectations and market standards by giving quality control procedures priority.

EGG COLLECTION AND HANDLING PRACTICES

To preserve egg quality and increase productivity in quail farming, efficient methods for collecting and managing eggs are essential.

To ensure that freshly laid eggs are gathered as soon as possible, start by creating a consistent plan for egg collection—ideally numerous times each day. When collecting eggs, use sanitized and clean baskets or trays to avoid cross-contamination and breakage.

Egg quality and shelf life can be affected by even slight imperfections, so handle them carefully to prevent cracks or damage. During egg collection, check the eggs for cleanliness and inconsistencies like discoloration or irregularities in the shell. Remove any inappropriate eggs from the batch. Dates of manufacture and other pertinent information should be properly labeled on eggs to track their freshness and guarantee accurate inventory management.

To maintain freshness and stop bacterial growth, store eggs in a cold, dry place after collecting, like a refrigerator. Washing eggs can destroy their protective cuticle and increase the chance of contamination, so try not to do so unless essential. From egg collection to distribution, proper handling and storage procedures are necessary to preserve egg quality and satisfy consumer expectations.

PROMOTING QUAIL EGGS TO MAKE MONEY

Marketing tactics that work are essential to promoting quail eggs and optimizing revenues in the quail farming industry. Determine who your target market is and what their wants and preferences are before moving further.

To draw in health-conscious customers, emphasize the nutritional advantages of quail eggs, such as their higher protein content and lower cholesterol than chicken eggs.

To reach a larger audience, make use of a variety of marketing channels, including social media, online platforms, local businesses, farmers' markets, and stores. Make aesthetically pleasing branding and packaging that conveys quality and freshness to prospective buyers. Offer specials, rebates, or package discounts to entice customers to buy and promote recurring business.

To foster trust and loyalty, interact with customers with recipe ideas, educational information, and reviews. To make constant improvements to your goods and services, ask for feedback from your clients. Work together with nearby companies or eateries to widen your distribution network and raise your profile.

Keep abreast of consumer tastes and market changes so that you may modify your marketing tactics as necessary. Marketing quail eggs may be done profitably by focusing on customer satisfaction and putting a thorough marketing plan into action.

NOVELTIES IN THE PRODUCTION OF QUAIL EGGS

The productivity, quality, and efficiency of quail farming have all been greatly increased by innovations in quail egg production. Advancements in breeding techniques, such as selective breeding for desired qualities like egg size and production rate, have resulted in improved egg yields. Genetic advancements allow for better disease resistance and general quail health, leading to higher egg quality.

Automation and technology integration in quail farming operations have expedited activities such as feeding, egg collection, and environmental control. Automatic egg collection systems improve overall cleanliness and egg quality by minimizing egg handling and lowering labor costs.

The ideal climatic conditions for quail welfare and egg production are achieved by climate-controlled housing systems.

Additionally, improvements in nutrition and quail-specific feed formulations have maximized egg yield and quality. Research on nutrigenomics has shed light on how to best tailor quail diets for particular health advantages and egg qualities.

Eco-friendly agricultural techniques, like handling trash and implementing energy-saving methods, support environmental preservation and ensure the long-term sustainability of quail egg production.

Innovation and sustainability in the quail farming sector are driven by ongoing research and development in technologies and methods. Quail farmers can fulfill market needs, maintain their competitiveness, and increase their overall profitability and success by adopting these advancements.

CHAPTER EIGHT

PROMOTING AND RETAILING QUAIL GOODS

DETERMINE WHICH MARKETS TO TARGET WITH QUAIL PRODUCTS

Comprehending your intended audience is essential while operating a quail farming enterprise. It entails locating possible clients who are eager to buy quail items like meat and eggs. To identify the most promising market segments, one important step is conducting demographic research on factors like age, income level, and geography. Potential target customers could include, for instance, health-conscious people looking for different sources of protein or gourmet chefs looking for unusual ingredients.

Furthermore, you can customize your items to fit particular needs and preferences by researching consumer preferences and industry trends. Surveys and market research can give you useful information about consumer behavior, enabling you to modify your marketing plans.

To attract ecologically aware consumers, you may concentrate on producing and marketing organic-certified quail meat and eggs if there's a growing demand for quail products.

You can also reach more target markets by forming alliances or working together with nearby eateries, supermarkets, or health food stores. By placing your quail products on display in these locations, you might draw in clients who might not have known about quail farming previously. All things considered, to optimize the potential for sales and business success, identifying target markets requires careful study and strategic planning.

QUAIL PRODUCT PACKAGING AND BRANDING

To distinguish out in the cutthroat quail farming market, a strong brand identity is necessary. Creating a distinctive brand name, logo, and graphic components that capture the essence of your business product offerings is the first step. Customers who care about the environment may relate to your farm, for example, if it emphasizes organic farming and sustainability. In this case, using eco-friendly packaging materials and emphasizing these features in your branding may help you reach this demographic.

Attracting clients and communicating the caliber of your quail items are greatly aided by the packaging. Putting money into expertly designed, aesthetically pleasing, and informational packaging can raise the perceived worth of your goods.

Customers can be reassured by clear labeling that includes nutritional data, production techniques, and certifications like organic or free-range.

Additionally, incorporating storytelling into your branding can help you connect emotionally with your target audience. By showcasing your quail farm's story and offering behind-the-scenes glimpses or client testimonials, you can personalize your company and foster loyalty. Reinforcing brand familiarity and promoting repeat purchases are two benefits of consistent branding across all touchpoints, from packaging to internet presence.

PRICING TECHNIQUES FOR QUAIL EGGS AND MEAT

Finding the ideal price for your quail products means striking a balance between market competitiveness and profitability. Setting a baseline pricing can be aided by performing a cost analysis that accounts for overhead, packaging costs, and production costs.

To support your price plan, think about how much people think your quail meat and eggs are worth in comparison to those of your rivals in the market.

Offer tiered pricing to accommodate a range of consumer preferences by differentiating your prices depending on product variations, such as organic or free-range options. Customers might be encouraged to buy more by bundling products or by offering incentives like discounts for large purchases, which can increase sales volume.

Furthermore, temporary promotions or seasonal price changes can generate urgency and boost sales during periods of high demand.

To be competitive, keep a close eye on market trends and competition pricing, and modify your price approach as necessary. Target consumers can provide insightful input on how they perceive prices and their willingness to pay by participating in price tests or surveys. To maximize profits and uphold customer satisfaction, pricing strategy, and perceived value must be balanced.

CHANNELS OF DISTRIBUTION FOR QUAIL PRODUCTS

Reaching target consumers and optimizing sales prospects for quail products depend on choosing the appropriate distribution channels. Customers looking for fresh and locally sourced items can reach you directly through traditional channels like specialty food stores, grocery stores, and local farmers' markets.

Forming alliances with these platforms might aid in raising awareness and drawing clients.

Beyond your local market, there are further options to reach a larger audience through online distribution channels. By setting up an online store or collaborating with marketplaces, clients can easily buy quail products from any location. Digital marketing techniques and social media platforms can increase traffic to your online store and lead generation.

To reach new clientele, consider investigating distribution alliances with eateries, caterers, and food service suppliers. Providing companies with options for bulk or wholesale pricing might encourage greater buys and build enduring connections.

Sustainable growth and expansion require regular evaluation and optimization of distribution networks based on consumer input and market trends.

MARKETING STRATEGIES FOR BUSINESSES THAT FARM QUAIL

To reach and engage target audiences, promoting your quail farming business effectively calls for a combination of traditional and digital marketing strategies. By using social media sites like Facebook, Instagram, and Twitter, you may interact with clients directly, provide farm updates, and exhibit your products. Creating and sharing aesthetically pleasing content, like cooking demonstrations, recipe ideas, or farm visits, can draw in fans and increase brand recognition.

Working along with food and lifestyle bloggers or influencers will help you reach a wider audience and gain credibility for your Quail product endorsements. Hosting competitions, freebies, or promotions on social media can create excitement and encourage user-generated content, providing organic visibility and interaction. Make use of geotagging and hashtags to expand your reach and attract local clients.

Conventional marketing strategies, like going to food festivals, trade exhibitions, or agricultural fairs, can help you network and expose more people to your products. By distributing leaflets, brochures, or product samples at neighborhood gatherings or forming alliances with like-minded companies, you can draw in more clients and increase foot traffic to your farm or retail stores. You may optimize brand exposure and sales growth for your quail farming business by putting into practice a thorough promotional strategy that integrates offline and online approaches.

CHAPTER NINE

COMPLIANCE WITH LAWS AND REGULATIONS

COMPREHENDING QUAIL FARMING REGULATIONS

The laws governing this agricultural industry must be understood to launch a profitable quail farming operation. The first step is to learn about the local regulations that apply to quail farming in your area. These rules and guidelines differ according to the place. Zoning laws, agricultural licenses, and adherence to animal care guidelines are a few examples of this.

Getting the required licenses and permissions is one of the most important parts of regulation. Usually, this entails applying to the appropriate government organizations in charge of agriculture or animal husbandry.

Documentation such as a business strategy, site inspection, and evidence of adherence to health and safety regulations may be needed for the procedure.

Understanding the rules also entails keeping up with any modifications or advancements in the sector. This could be going to seminars, becoming a member of associations for farmers, or getting advice from attorneys who focus on agricultural law. You can make sure that your quail farming business is both legally sound and long-lasting by remaining aware and compliant.

REQUIREMENTS FOR PERMITS AND LICENSES

Starting and running a quail farm requires obtaining licenses and permits. You might require a variety of approvals, including company licenses, permits for animal welfare, and agricultural zoning, depending on where you live. These licenses serve as proof that your quail farming business conforms with all applicable local laws and ordinances.

You'll probably need to submit extensive paperwork to get these permissions, such as a business plan detailing your farming methods, waste management strategies, animal welfare procedures, and biosecurity measures.

To make sure that your farm complies with health and safety regulations, you might also need to submit to site inspections.

To minimize delays in starting your quail farm, you must begin the licensing and permit process as early as possible in the planning phase. You may expedite the permitting process and guarantee that your farm runs within legal bounds by collaborating closely with regulatory agencies and consulting with seasoned farmers or agricultural experts.

OBSERVANCE OF SAFETY AND HEALTH REGULATIONS

In quail farming, adherence to health and safety regulations is mandatory. This entails keeping quail housing clean and hygienic, putting biosecurity measures in place to stop illness outbreaks, and giving your quail enough food and medical attention.

You must create a thorough farm management plan that covers matters like waste management, pest control, vaccination schedules, and emergency response procedures to abide by health and safety regulations. Regular inspections and audits may also be required to verify continued compliance.

Maintaining high standards for health and safety requires educating your employees on how to handle and care for quail, enforcing stringent cleanliness regulations, and keeping thorough records of all farm operations.

By giving these factors top priority, you not only comply with regulations but also advance the health and welfare of your flock of quail.

CONSIDERING THE ENVIRONMENTAL IMPACT

Like any agricultural practice, raising quail has an impact on the environment that needs to be carefully studied and maintained. This entails taking care of matters like land conservation, water management, waste management, and reducing pollution from farming activities.

You can lessen the environmental effect of your quail farm by implementing sustainable farming techniques including rotational grazing, water-efficient irrigation systems, and composting quail excrement for fertilizer. Sustainability can be further improved by implementing technology like eco-friendly packaging materials and renewable energy sources.

It's critical to regularly carry out environmental effect assessments and modify your agricultural methods as necessary. Your quail farm may run in harmony with the environment if you interact with local conservation authorities, take part in eco-certification programs, and stay up to date on best practices for agriculture.

RISK CONTROL AND INSURANCE FOR QUAIL FARMS

Running a quail farm requires careful planning and risk management because these measures guard your investment and reduce the possibility of financial loss. Insurance types to think about include liability insurance for accidents or lawsuits, property insurance to cover farm buildings and equipment, and livestock insurance to guard against losses due to disease or predation.

Identifying possible risks, such as disease outbreaks, natural disasters, and market swings, and putting policies in place to lessen them are all part of risk management techniques for quail farms. This could entail following biosecurity procedures, varying sources of income, keeping emergency cash on hand, and putting backup plans in place.

You may evaluate the unique insurance requirements of your farm and create a risk management strategy that fits by speaking with insurance experts who specialize in agricultural coverage. Your quail farm is safe and robust against unforeseen obstacles thanks to routine evaluations and updates of your risk management plans and insurance coverage.

CHAPTER TEN

GROWING YOUR BUSINESS IN QUAIL FARMING

INCREASING CAPABILITIES FOR QUAIL PRODUCTION

To keep up with the increasing demand, you must strategically plan and execute the expansion of your quail production capabilities. Start by evaluating the space, tools, and resources that are currently available in your setup.

Determine what needs to be improved and expanded, such as the number of quail pens, the equipment for effective water and feed management, and the breeding procedures.

Next, create a staged expansion strategy to guarantee steady growth and prevent overstretching your resources. This could entail constructing brand-new quail housing units, making an automated feeding and watering system investment, and putting biosecurity protocols in place to stop disease outbreaks. Seek advice on optimum techniques and possible obstacles from seasoned quail farmers or agricultural specialists.

Lastly, keep a close eye on your expansion's development and analyze it frequently to make the required corrections and enhancements. Maintain thorough documentation of all production metrics, expenses, and income to evaluate the profitability of your growing business. You can boost your quail production capacities while upholding the highest levels of quality and efficiency by meticulously organizing and carrying out your expansion plan.

PARTNERSHIPS AND OUTSOURCING FOR DEVELOPMENT

You can focus on your core skills and streamline operations by outsourcing some parts of your quail farming business. Think about contracting out to specialist organizations or contractors for duties like marketing, equipment maintenance, and feed manufacturing.

By doing this, you may take advantage of their knowledge and assets while freeing up time and resources for other crucial areas.

Partnerships with distributors, suppliers, or other farms can also generate potential for expansion and synergy. Work together with feed providers to get affordable prices and dependable delivery times. Join forces with neighborhood shops or eateries to create a reliable sales channel for your quail merchandise. Investigate partnership opportunities with nearby farms to pool resources and increase combined output capacity.

Keep open lines of communication and mutually beneficial arrangements with collaborators and outsourcing partners. Review and evaluate these alliances regularly to make sure they're still helping your company flourish. You may improve your quail farming business's scalability and sustainability by utilizing outside resources and developing strategic connections.

EMPLOYING AND EDUCATING QUAIL FARM WORKERS

A knowledgeable workforce is essential to the efficient running and expansion of your quail farm. Establish roles and responsibilities for breeders, caretakers, administrative staff, and sales professionals based on the needs of your farm. To draw in qualified applicants, clearly explain the job requirements, qualifications, and performance criteria.

Prioritize hiring those who have a great interest in quail farming or who have relevant experience. Make sure the people you interview and background check are in line with the principles and objectives of your farm. New personnel should receive thorough training and continuous assistance to acquaint them with farm operations, safety procedures, and animal care techniques.

By offering workshops, seminars, and on-the-job training, you may support your employees' ongoing education and skill development.

Encourage an environment at work where creativity, teamwork, and communication are valued. To encourage development and accountability, evaluate employee performance regularly and offer constructive criticism. By making investments in your quail farm employees, you can create a knowledgeable and driven group that enhances the performance of your enterprise.

BUDGETING AND FINANCIAL PLANNING

For quail farming to be profitable and grow sustainably, budgeting and financial planning must be done well. Begin by carefully examining every aspect of your existing financial status, including your income, expenses, assets, and liabilities. Determine your areas of strength and room for development so that you may make informed budgetary decisions.

Create a comprehensive budget that accounts for all expenditures associated with quail farming operations, including feed, veterinary care, equipment upkeep, labor costs, and marketing charges. Strategically distribute finances according to priorities, seasonality, and projected income sources. Include backup plans and emergency cash to reduce unanticipated costs or difficulties.

Keep a close eye on your financial performance and compare it to your budget estimates regularly to spot any differences and make the required corrections. To maximize your financial plans and investment choices, consult agricultural economists or financial experts. For the sake of financial reporting, grant applications, and tax compliance, keep accurate records and documentation. You can guarantee your quail farming business's financial stability and longevity by implementing sound financial management practices.

EXPANDING THE RANGE OF QUAIL GOODS AND SERVICES

Expanding the range of your quail offerings can bring in more money and draw in a larger clientele. To find possible prospects for product diversification, start by evaluating market developments, consumer preferences, and rival products.

Think of branching out into value-added items like quail eggs, meat products, feathers, and fertilizer in addition to live quail sales.

Make research and development investments to create novel quail-based products or enhance current ones. Work together with product developers, chefs, and nutritionists to generate original recipes, designs for packaging, and advertising campaigns. Investigate specialist shops or niche marketplaces that serve gourmet cooks, health-conscious shoppers, and pet owners who are interested in exotic animals.

Use industry events, internet platforms, and focused marketing campaigns to advertise your variety of quail products and services. To appeal to environmentally conscious consumers, emphasize the nutritional benefits, sustainable techniques, and ethical farming standards of your products. To improve your product offers and maintain your competitiveness in the quail farming sector, keep an eye on consumer feedback and market demand.

CHAPTER ELEVEN

UPCOMING DEVELOPMENTS AND TRENDS

NEW TECHNOLOGY IN QUAIL PRODUCTION

Emerging technologies are transforming conventional quail farming methods and opening doors to more sustainable and productive enterprises. One example of this technology is automated feeding systems, which guarantee accurate feeding schedules and lower labor expenses while producing healthier and more productive quails.

These systems can be set up to distribute feed in predetermined amounts and at predetermined times, which maximizes growth and reduces waste.

Additionally, quail farm settings have been greatly enhanced by developments in climate control technology. To create the ideal environment for quail growth and egg production, smart sensors keep an eye on temperature, humidity, and ventilation. This degree of management lowers the population of quail's risk of stress-related health problems while simultaneously increasing output.

Moreover, genetic technologies are essential to contemporary quail farming. Genetic markers are used in selective breeding programs to improve desirable qualities like disease resistance, egg production, and meat quality. Higher yields and improved overall performance are the outcomes of this focused strategy, which meets consumer demand for high-quality quail goods.

ECO-FRIENDLY METHODS FOR QUAIL FARMS

Farmers raising quail are implementing strategies that balance profitability and environmental responsibility as sustainability becomes a top priority. A crucial component is waste management, where cutting-edge approaches like quail dung composting are becoming more and more popular. Composted manure is a nutrient-rich fertilizer that improves soil health and lessens the demand for synthetic substitutes.

Furthermore, a key component of contemporary quail farming is sustainable feed procurement. In an effort to reduce their dependency on chemical additives and minimize the carbon footprint associated with transportation, farmers are increasingly using locally produced and organic feeds. This is advantageous for the environment as well as customers looking for quail items made responsibly.

Practices that conserve water are also essential to sustainable quail farming. Drip irrigation systems and rainfall collection are examples of technologies that help farms reduce water use while maintaining crop and quail hydration levels. These methods support long-term farm viability and cost savings in addition to protecting a valuable resource.

CONSUMER PREFERENCES AND MARKET TRENDS

A thorough understanding of consumer tastes and market trends is essential for success in the quail farming sector. The growing popularity of organic and free-range quail products is one noteworthy development. Farmers are adopting organic certification and free-range agricultural practices as a result of consumers' growing demand for ethically produced products.

Furthermore, quail is becoming more and more popular as a sustainable source of protein. Consumers who are concerned about the environment and animal welfare find quail to be appealing due to their efficient feed conversion rate and less ecological footprint. Farmers now have the chance to promote quail products as more eco-friendly substitutes for conventional chicken in light of this trend.

In addition, the growing number of health-conscious consumers has raised the market for quail meat and eggs because of their nutritious value. Compared to other meats, quail products are lower in fat and cholesterol and higher in protein, vitamins, and minerals. By leveraging these health-conscious tendencies, quail farms can get a competitive edge in the market.

RESEARCH OPPORTUNITIES AND EDUCATIONAL INITIATIVES

Research and educational programs are essential to the development of the quail farming sector. Innovations in disease control, breeding methods, and sustainable farming practices are the result of partnerships between academic institutions, farms, and agriculture organizations. These programs help the quail farming industry as a whole, in addition to the farmers that participate in it.

There are lots of chances for research in fields including disease resistance, genetic enhancement, and feed optimization. Farmers may take advantage of new opportunities and keep ahead of industry issues by investing in research and development. Programs for education also provide aspiring and new farmers with the information and abilities they need to be successful in quail farming.

Furthermore, collaborations with governmental bodies and business associations promote the sharing of best practices and the exchange of expertise. Workshops, seminars, and training courses offer insightful information about the most recent developments and legal specifications, guaranteeing that quail farmers do their business ethically and efficiently.

WORLDWIDE PROSPECTS FOR QUAIL FARMING ENTERPRISES

Businesses seeking to increase their market share can consider the potential worldwide opportunities that quail farming offers. Export markets present profitable opportunities for quail products, especially in areas where quail eggs and meat are regarded as staple foods or delicacies. Creating international trade alliances can lead to the creation of new sources of income for farms and their diversification.

Furthermore, the export of quail products to far-off markets is made easier by technical developments in logistics and transportation. By maintaining product freshness and quality during transportation, cold chain management satisfies both client demands and strict international requirements. With this smooth supply chain integration, quail growers can confidently meet demand around the world.

Additionally, the dynamics of the worldwide quail industry are influenced by cultural variety. Achieving success in international expansion requires a thorough understanding of local preferences, culinary traditions, and market trends in the target locations. Global brand exposure and competitiveness are increased by strategic marketing and distribution plans customized for each market group.

CHAPTER TWELVE

FAQS & FREQUENTLY ASKED QUESTIONS

TAKING CARE OF QUAIL EGGS

Because quail eggs are fragile, managing them carefully is necessary to preserve their quality and safety. It's crucial to handle quail eggs carefully when gathering them to prevent breaking or harming the shells. To avoid contamination, use hands that are dry and clean. To cushion the eggs and keep them from breaking while being transported or stored, place them in a clean container lined with soft material.

Once gathered, keep the quail eggs out of direct sunlight in a cool, dry location. Washing the eggs can destroy their natural protective coating and increase the danger of contamination, so try not to do so unless essential. If washing is required, wash with warm water and a little detergent, rinse well, and pat dry with a fresh cloth. Quail eggs are preserved for extended periods when handled and stored properly.

Make sure quail eggs are boiled all the way through before consuming them to get rid of any possible bacteria or infections. Quail eggs are comparable to chicken eggs in that they can be boiled, fried, or poached; but, because of their smaller size, quail eggs cook more quickly than chicken eggs. A safe and satisfying culinary experience is ensured by handling and preparing quail eggs properly.

TYPICAL QUAIL ILLNESSES AND THEIR TREATMENTS

Diseases such as respiratory infections, parasite infestations, and nutritional deficits can affect quails. Symptoms such as nasal discharge, coughing, and sneezing can be brought on by respiratory infections. Egg production can be reduced, weight loss can occur, and feather loss can result from parasitic infestations like worms or mites. Inadequate nutrition might cause stunted growth, fragile eggshells, or decreased fertility.

To prevent and treat common infections in quails, maintain good hygiene in their living and nesting grounds. To lower the risk of respiratory illnesses, give the coop regular cleaning and disinfection, change the bedding frequently, and make sure there is adequate ventilation. Regularly check on the health of quails to look for symptoms of disease, such as alterations in behavior, hunger, or egg production.

Consult a veterinarian for advice on the best medications or supportive treatment for respiratory illnesses. Certain drugs or natural therapies, such as diatomaceous earth for external parasites, can be used to treat parasitic infections. To avoid nutritional deficits, make sure quails have access to a balanced diet high in vitamins, minerals, and protein.

PROFITABILITY OF QUAIL FARMING FOR NOVICES

For novices, quail farming can be financially rewarding with the right preparation, oversight, and market analysis. To begin with, find out how much the market is willing to pay for quail items like meat, eggs, and feathers.

Determine prospective clients, such as eateries, grocery stores, and individual buyers, to assess market prospects and price tactics.

Determine the initial investment costs for the quail's home, gear, feed, and initial stock. To assess possible returns on investment, take into account variables like breed selection, production capacity, and operating costs. Employ cost-effective and productivity-boosting agricultural techniques, such as improving feed conversion ratios, taking preventative steps against disease, and setting up effective egg collection methods.

Explore value-added items like quail egg products, and feathers for crafts, or provide agritourism experiences like farm tours or workshops to diversify your revenue streams. Maintaining long-term success in quail farming requires you to constantly evaluate and modify your farming tactics in response to consumer feedback, market trends, and profitability analyses.

IDEAL COMPOSITION OF QUAIL FEED

A well-balanced food is essential for the growth, egg production, and general health of quails. A combination of grains, protein sources, vitamins, and minerals make up the perfect quail diet composition. Start with a commercial quail feed that is specially designed to meet the nutritional requirements of quail, or make your custom feed blend according to advice from experts.

Grain such as corn, wheat, or millet is a common energy source in quail feed. Protein sources that include critical amino acids for muscle growth and egg production include soybean meal, fish meal, and insect meal. Add sources of calcium to your diet, such as limestone or crushed oyster shells, for strong eggshells and healthy bones.

Add vitamins and minerals to the diet, particularly the B-complex, D3, E, and A vitamins, as well as minerals like potassium, phosphorus, and calcium. Quails require fresh, clean water at all times for proper digestion, egg production, and general hydration. Observe how much feed the quail is consuming and modify the amounts according to their growth phases and desired output.

EFFECTIVE QUAIL PRODUCT MARKETING

To reach target clients and promote quail products, effective marketing methods are essential. To set your items apart from the competition, start by determining your USPs, which could include specialty quail breeds, greater product quality, or organic farming methods. Create a captivating brand narrative that highlights the advantages of quail products and connects with your target market.

Make use of both offline and online marketing platforms to expand your audience. To promote your quail products, provide informative articles about quail farming, and interact with customers via blogs, social media, and email newsletters, create a polished website or online store. To raise brand awareness and draw in new clients, use digital marketing strategies including influencer alliances, social media advertising, and search engine optimization (SEO).

Participating in local events, culinary festivals, or farmers' markets is one way to promote and sell your quail products to customers directly through offline marketing techniques. To increase your market reach and distribution channels, work with distributors, restaurants, and specialized shops. To establish credibility and trust, gather client comments, evaluations, and testimonials. Then, keep your marketing tactics up to date by incorporating consumer preferences and market trends into ongoing strategy innovations.

www.ingramcontent.com/pod-product-compliance
Lightning Source LLC
Chambersburg PA
CBHW071836210526
45479CB00001B/158